IN ONE EAR &
OUT THE OTHER

ANTONIA BRICO
& her amazingly musical life

An Amazing Women Series biography by DIANE WORTHEY

penny
candy
BOOKS

Penny Candy Books

Oklahoma City & Greensboro

Text © 2020 Diane Worthey

Illustrations © 2020 Morgana Wallace

All rights reserved. Published 2020. Printed in Canada.

 This book is printed on paper certified to the environmental and social standards of the Forest Stewardship Council™ (FSC®).

Photo of Diane Worthey: Jenny Bowles

Design: Shanna Compton

ISBN-13: 978-1-7342259-1-4 (hardcover)

Small press. Big conversations.

www.pennycandybooks.com

Library of Congress Cataloging-in-Publication Data

Names: Worthey, Diane, author. | Wallace, Morgana, illustrator.
Title: In one ear and out the other : Antonia Brico & her amazingly musical
   life / [text] Diane Worthey ; [illustrations] Morgana Wallace.
Description: Oklahoma City : Penny Candy Books, 2020. | Series: The amazing
   women series | Includes bibliographical references. | Audience: Ages
   7-11 | Audience: Grades 4-6
Identifiers: LCCN 2020012851 | ISBN 9781734225914 (hardcover)
Subjects: LCSH: Brico, Antonia--Juvenile literature. | Conductors
   (Music)--United States--Biography--Juvenile literature.
Classification: LCC ML3930.B8 W67 22020 | DDC 784.2092 [B]--dc23
LC record available at https://lccn.loc.gov/2020012851

24 23 22 21 20   1 2 3 4 5

For Antonia

Chapter 1

One spring day at a concert in San Francisco's Lakeside Park, Wilhelmina Wolthuis fell under the spell of the conductor's magic wand. With the flick of his baton, flutes trilled. Cymbals crashed. Bass drums boomed. Wilhelmina sat amazed at what one little stick could do. She, too, wanted a magic wand. And so, at age twelve, her dream began.

It was 1914. Only a handful of women had ever stepped onto a podium to lead an orchestra with their batons. Girls were told they couldn't become conductors. But Wilhelmina didn't listen to discouraging words. They went in one ear and out the other.

After the concert, Wilhelmina followed the conductor from Lakeside Park around San Francisco on streetcars until he noticed her. The conductor agreed to give her piano lessons but told her that women couldn't conduct. Wilhelmina loved her piano. She delighted in practicing long hours. But she couldn't stop thinking about that baton!

The conductor's words went in one ear and out the other.

Chapter 2

In high school, as Wilhelmina was making plans to go to music school, she discovered a painful secret: she was shocked to learn that her birth name was not Wilhelmina. Mr. and Mrs. Wolthuis explained that she was named Antonia Louisa Brico by her birth mother. They were her foster parents, and they didn't want to support her any longer. Shattered, Wilhelmina left home. Somehow, she would chase her dream on her own.

Wilhelmina enrolled herself at the University of California, Berkeley. To pay tuition, she took a job at the local dime store where she played the piano in the front window for customers as they shopped. Wilhelmina dazzled the audience with her lightning-fast fingers. Up and down the keyboard they flew! But still her desire burned. She wanted to become a conductor of a great orchestra.

Determined as ever, Wilhelmina worked as an usher for the San Francisco Symphony. She couldn't afford a good seat, so she brought her own. People stared, but Wilhelmina did not care. With musical scores on her lap, she studied the conductor's technique.

Over and over, important men told her that women couldn't be conductors. Her friend told her that if she took the podium to conduct, the audience would throw rotten eggs at her.

Wilhelmina wasn't listening. The words went in one ear and out the other.

Chapter 3

In 1924, Wilhelmina accepted a scholarship to study piano with a famous New York conductor. Wilhelmina still loved the piano, but she *yearned* to conduct. She would tell her new teacher about her plans. Maybe he would listen. Her piano was loaded onto a steamship, and she sailed to New York.

Upon her arrival, she reclaimed her birth name and became . . . Antonia Brico once again.

"You have talent, Antonia, but nobody wants a woman conductor," her teacher said.

Undeterred, Antonia secretly enrolled in conducting lessons and didn't tell him. When he found out, he was furious!

Chapter 4

After searching for years for *someone* to believe in her, Antonia met a renowned yogi, Yogananda, who told her that she would become a great conductor. His faith in her was so strong that he paid her way to Germany so she could audition for the Master School of Conducting at the Berlin State Academy of Music, and she was admitted.

For the first time *ever*, an American would graduate from the finest conducting school in the world. Antonia's smile reached from ear to ear. Finally, her dream of becoming a great conductor was coming true. At last, Antonia had her own magic wand.

But, while her male colleagues began to enjoy international success, Antonia learned that no one would sponsor a concert led by a woman!

So, she sponsored her *own* fabulous debut and approached the podium with gusto.

The silky tones of the Berlin Philharmonic rang in Antonia's ear and in her heart. She wanted a full-time position as conductor of a major orchestra, but no one would give her one. It was 1930, and as a woman, she could only be a *guest* conductor.

Berliner Herold

Male conductors in Germany had much to learn from this glorious young woman

Guest conducts the Los Angeles Philharmonic at the Hollywood Bowl to rave reviews

New York Times

Miss Antonia Brico of San Francisco, the first American woman to conduct a concert in Berlin, made a successful debut tonight in Berlin with the Philharmonic Orchestra, which followed her baton most enthusiastically in Dvorak's Symphony in D minor, eliciting thunderous applause.

Chapter 5

In 1932, Antonia escaped Germany, where the Nazis had taken control, and returned to New York. There, nine women asked Antonia to form an ensemble for them. They had no place to play because only men could perform in professional orchestras.

"If nine, why not ninety?" Antonia asked. Antonia met with Eleanor Roosevelt, the wife of the president of the United States, to gather financial support to build a full orchestra of professional women. In 1935, the New York Women's Symphony Orchestra was born. The orchestra performed to great acclaim at Carnegie Hall and brought down the house with applause.

Antonia's work with the New York Women's Symphony Orchestra was a huge success. Now women musicians were being taken seriously! Soon, Antonia was invited to guest-conduct the New York Philharmonic, the oldest professional orchestra in the United States. No woman had ever led this world-class orchestra of men.

On July 25, 1938, Antonia Brico stepped up to lead the New York Philharmonic. Antonia rapped her baton on the podium for silence. Then, as she raised her magic wand, one hundred men followed her lead.

Antonia was happy that women were being noticed as capable musicians, but Antonia wanted something more. Antonia wanted women and men to make music *together*.

In 1939, Antonia set out to change the New York Women's Symphony Orchestra to a mixed-gender orchestra. The symphony board disagreed. They did not approve of Antonia's idea to have women and men play music alongside each other. They feared no one would buy tickets. "There are no more opportunities for you here," they said.

Antonia hid her heartache.
No one saw her tears.
    She decided to let the
discouraging words go
in one car and out
the other as she
kept searching
for a way to
reach her
dream.

Chapter 6

And then the Denver Symphony offered Antonia a guest-conducting job. Crowds packed the auditorium.

The Mile High City seemed to be welcoming Antonia.

She tried to audition for a permanent opening with the Denver Civic Orchestra, but they rejected her application.

Chapter 7

Finally, when Antonia was forty-five, the Denver Businessmen's Orchestra, a semiprofessional orchestra, wanted Antonia as their permanent conductor. Antonia was happy to conduct the pieces she loved, but the orchestra only performed five concerts a *year*. She was starving for more.

Because Antonia had bills to pay, she taught piano lessons to promising young musicians, inspiring them to reach high. A former student made a documentary film about Antonia's life. The film was nominated for an Academy Award! For a brief time, Antonia enjoyed her newfound fame. Yet professional conducting jobs never came.

Chapter 8

During Antonia's lifetime, the world was not ready to embrace women as conductors. But . . . Antonia's life broke barriers, sweeping the curtain open!

Young, talented women are in the wings. Standing on the shoulders of Antonia, it is their time to shine. Inspired by Antonia's grit, they step up to the podium with their own magic wands. Today, women such as Marin Alsop, JoAnn Falletta, and Han-Na Chang lead the world's greatest orchestras . . .

. . . because Antonia Brico let the words "Women can't be conductors!" go in one ear . . . and out the other.

TIMELINE OF ANTONIA'S AMAZINGLY MUSICAL LIFE

1902	1904	1912	c.1914	c.1918	1919

1902
Antonia Louisa Brico is born to a poor cleaning woman in Rotterdam, Holland. At two days old, her mother gives her to a convent.

1904
Mr. and Mrs. Wolthuis, a baker and his wife, take Antonia in as a foster child. Antonia's aunt later tries to reclaim her, but Mr. and Mrs. Wolthuis flee with Antonia to San Francisco, California, changing Antonia's name to "Wilhelmina."

1912
Wilhelmina begins piano lessons upon advice of a doctor, to cure her nail-biting habit.

c.1914
Wilhelmina attends band concerts in the park with her choral teacher, Mrs. Minnie Davis Wadsworth. After seeing Paul Steindorff conduct, Wilhelmina decides to become a conductor. She follows Maestro Steindorff around on streetcars to attempt to meet him.

c.1918
During an argument with her foster mother, Wilhelmina learns the truth about her birth. She is told that she is no longer wanted. She leaves home and stays with friends until she graduates from college.

1919
Wilhelmina enrolls herself at the University of California, Berkeley to study piano with Paul Steindorff.

1923	1924	c.1925	1926	1927	1929

Wilhelmina graduates with honors from the University of California, Berkeley.

The spiritual leader Yogananda tells her that she will become a great conductor. She returns to California to study piano with Modeste Alloo.

Yogananda pays Antonia's way to Germany. She is admitted to the Master School of Conducting at the Berlin State Academy of Music, University of Berlin, and studies conducting with Dr. Karl Muck.

Wilhelmina Wolthuis reclaims her name as Antonia Brico. She sails to New York via the Panama Canal to study with pianist Sigismond Stojowski.

Antonia travels to Holland to meet her birth relatives. Her mother is no longer living, but she meets uncles, aunts, and cousins.

Antonia becomes the first American to graduate from the Master School of Conducting at the Berlin State Academy of Music, University of Berlin.

| 1930 | 1931 | 1932 | 1934–35 | 1937 | 1938 |

Antonia conducts the Berlin Philharmonic and the Los Angeles Philharmonic at the Hollywood Bowl.

Antonia leaves Europe to escape the Nazi regime. She moves to New York with no prospects of work.

Antonia travels to Finland to meet and study with Jean Sibelius. She begins a lifelong friendship with the famous composer.

Antonia guest-conducts the Warsaw Philharmonic, the Hamburg Symphony, the Latvia State Orchestra, and conducts a concert for Queen Elizabeth of Belgium in Brussels. She conducts many more orchestras as a guest conductor.

Antonia meets with Eleanor Roosevelt at the White House to gather sponsorships to start the New York Women's Symphony Orchestra. The orchestra features over 100 women. They perform at Carnegie Hall to great acclaim.

Antonia becomes the first woman to conduct the New York Philharmonic on July 25, 1938 at Lewisohn Stadium, Manhattan, New York

1939	1940	1942	1946	1947	1947

Antonia disbands the New York Women's Symphony Orchestra to form a mixed-gender orchestra. Named the Brico Symphony, the ensemble is the first of its kind in the United States and is featured at the 1939 New York World's Fair. After a short season, the board refuses to support a mixed-gender orchestra and pulls all financial support. Antonia is unemployed.

Antonia moves to Denver, Colorado. She teaches private conducting, piano and voice lessons and guest-conducts the Denver Symphony Orchestra for the second time. She wants to audition for conductor of the Denver Civic Orchestra but they reject her application because of her gender.

A semiprofessional orchestra, the Denver Businessmen's Orchestra, asks Antonia to become their permanent conductor. She accepts.

Antonia is awarded the Pro-Finlandia gold medal for the successful concerts she conducts in Finland.

Antonia guest-conducts the Helsinki State Symphony honoring her friend Jean Sibelius. She also guest-conducts the London Philharmonic and creates the Denver Bach Society.

Antonia guest-conducts the Denver Symphony Orchestra in Denver, Colorado, and the National Symphony Orchestra in Washington, DC.

| 1950 | 1951–67 | 1973 | 1974–85 | 1989 |

Antonia studies Bach with Albert Schweitzer, becomes his friend, and helps in his clinic in Lambaréné, in French Equatorial Africa.

Judy Collins, (Antonia's former piano student and famous folk singer) and Jill Godmilow make the film *Antonia: A Portrait of the Woman*. When released in 1974, the film is nominated for an Academy Award.

Antonia dies, having never fulfilled her dream of a becoming a full-time conductor of a major symphony orchestra. Standing on the shoulders of Antonia, more women conductors step up to the podium and are accepted as leaders.

Antonia perseveres but is not hired by professional orchestras. The Denver Businessmen's Orchestra changes its name to the Brico Symphony in her honor.

Antonia continues to conduct the Brico Symphony. The success of the documentary film made by Collins and Godmilow gives Antonia short-lived invitations to conduct the world's greatest orchestras and a return engagement at the Los Angeles Hollywood Bowl.

THREE OF TODAY'S WOMEN CONDUCTORS

JoAnn Falletta as born in Queens, New York, in 1954. She began studying classical guitar at the age of seven, later performing with the New York Philharmonic and other major orchestras. By the time she was eleven years old, Maestra Falletta knew she had a second musical love: the baton. At Mannes College, Maestra Falletta's desire to learn to conduct grew. Degrees in conducting from Mannes and Juilliard followed. In 1991, Maestra Falletta stepped onto the podium of the Virginia Symphony Orchestra to take the lead. In 1999, Maestra Falletta became the Music Director of the Buffalo Philharmonic Orchestra. Additional highlights of her conducting career include positions with the Brevard Music Center, the Ulster Orchestra, the Long Beach Symphony Orchestra and the Women's Philharmonic. Maestra Falletta has won several Grammy Awards for her recordings with leading record labels. She also has appeared in many television and radio spots, including the PBS TV documentary by Penn and Teller, *Behind the Scenes, Vol. 3: Music and Dance*. Maestra Falletta, also an avid writer, has published a book of her own poetry, *Love Letters to Music*, in which she describes her innermost experiences as a classical musician and conductor. For more information visit www.joannfalletta.com.

Marin Alsop, born in New York City in 1956, began piano lessons at age two and violin lessons at age five. By seven, she was attending the Pre-College division of the Juilliard School and later earned degrees in violin performance at Juilliard. In 1965, when Maestra Alsop was nine, she watched Leonard Bernstein conduct the New York Philharmonic. Like Antonia Brico, she was inspired by a conductor's "magic wand" and knew she wanted to become a conductor. In 1985, Maestra Alsop became a conducting student of Harold Farberman. Her own conducting career began to blossom in 1989 when she became the first woman to receive the Koussevitzky Conducting Prize at Tanglewood Music Center. In 1993, four years after Antonia Brico's passing, Maestra Alsop was named Music Director of the Colorado Symphony (Denver). In 2007, Maestra Alsop stepped up to the podium as Director of the Baltimore Symphony. In 2013, she became Principal Conductor of the São Paulo Symphony Orchestra. Maestra Alsop's 2019 appointment as Chief Conductor of the ORF Vienna Radio Symphony Orchestra makes her the first woman to lead a Viennese Orchestra. For more information visit www.marinalsop.com.

Han-Na Chang, born in South Korea in 1982, studied piano and cello as a young child. In 1993, she moved with her family to the United States and continued her studies as a student at the Pre-College Division of Julliard. In 1994, her musical career propelled forward when, after only five years of study on the cello, she won the International Rostropovich Cello Competition. Recording contracts and cello performances with world class orchestras, including the London Philharmonic, filled Maestra Chang's teenage years. Then, she became enamored with the podium while watching her cello teacher, Guiseppe Sinopoli, conduct. Maestra Chang dove fearlessly into conducting with James DePreist at Juilliard as her teacher. As she developed her newfound passion, Maestra Chang's love of Beethoven led her back to her birthplace of South Korea to make documentaries about the Beethoven Symphonies. Through these documentaries, Maestra Chang's talent as a conductor shone bright! Maestra Chang was appointed the Music Director of the Qatar Philharmonic in 2012. In 2017, she became the first female conductor to be named Chief Conductor of the Trondheim Symphony Orchestra. In addition to full time appointments, Maestra Chang has guest-conducted the Finnish Radio Symphony Orchestra, the Danish National Symphony Orchestra, the Minnesota Symphony Orchestra and the Tokyo Symphony Orchestra, to name a few. For more information visit www.harrisonparrott.com/artists/han-na-chang

Many more amazing women now enjoy full-time appointments with the world's greatest orchestras.

THREE WOMEN WHO PAVED THE WAY

Emma Steiner (1850–1928) rose to the podium in America in the late 1800s. Beginning at the tender age of seven, Maestra Steiner taught herself to sing, compose music, and conduct. Her family was not supportive of her aspirations. In the early 1900s, Maestra Steiner's expertise in conducting was noticed by the manager of the Metropolitan Opera House. Yet, the times did not accept women as conductors of major opera houses. The manager admitted he was not brave enough to offer her the job. Maestra Steiner appeared on thousands of lesser-known stages during her lifetime both as a singer and as the musical director of various operas. She became most known for conducting hundreds of performances of the opera *The Mikado* by Arthur Sullivan. In Maestra Steiner's later life, as she began to lose her eyesight, she moved to Nome, Alaska, with the intent of producing her own operas. Instead, she became a miner and a prospector! Her discovery of substantial tin deposits near Nome made Alaskan history.

Mary Wurm (1860-1938) was born in England, yet spent most of her life in Germany. Along with her sisters Matilde, Adela, and Alice, Maestra Wurm studied the piano as a young child. In college, she studied composition and piano at the Stuttgart Conservatory. During her studies, she became a piano student of Clara Schumann and studied composition with many famous teachers, including Carl Reinecke. On November 5, 1887, Maestra Wurm presented her own compositions as the piano soloist for the Berlin Philharmonic. During this concert, she became the first woman to conduct the all-male orchestra when she conducted the overture. In 1898, Maestra Wurm created a women's orchestra in Berlin. This professional-level orchestra traveled Europe, performing until 1900.

English born **Ethel Leginska** (1886–1970) showed great talent for the piano at an early age. She spent her childhood studying advanced piano repertoire in Frankfurt, Vienna, and Berlin. When she was sixteen, she made her first appearance as piano soloist with the

Queen's Hall Orchestra in London. In 1914, Maestra Leginska began to compose her own compositions. In 1918, she became a student of the famous composer, Ernest Bloch. Maestra Leginska's passion for conducting led her to study with Eugene Goossens and Robert Hager, men who believed women and men should share the podium. Maestra Leginska, a rebel of her time, dressed in practical concert clothes instead of long, flowing gowns. Maestra Leginska made history when she became the first woman to conduct the Los Angeles Philharmonic on August 4, 1925, at the Hollywood Bowl. Sadly, she was ultimately regarded as a novelty woman conductor, and her conducting career ended in 1935. Except for conducting a performance of her own opera *The Rose and the Ring* in 1957, Maestra Leginska spent the rest of her musical career teaching the piano in Los Angeles, California.

ACKNOWLEDGMENTS

Antonia Brico wanted to be known simply as a great conductor—not as a novelty woman conductor on the podium. I was fortunate to have played violin in the Brico Symphony (now the Denver Philharmonic) as a teenager in the 1980s. Dr. Brico never boasted about her accomplishments. Although she was heartbroken about never being offered a permanent appointment with a major symphony orchestra, she kept her heartache from showing. She was always focused on her passion of conducting great symphonic works. I learned much from her grit-filled example: Find a passion, work hard, believe in your dream. The art is what matters. Thank you Dr. Brico, for teaching me this.

Thank you also to:

My beloved husband, Guy, who lit the spark. Thank you for asking, "What about Antonia Brico?"

Alexis Orgera and Chad Reynolds at Penny Candy Books. A story needs the right publisher and editor to bring it to life. I can't imagine more noble human beings to work with than the two of you. I will never forget this journey. I am forever grateful.

Shanna Compton for the beautiful timeline design and layout of the book which allowed me to tell a more complete story of Antonia Brico's life.

Barbara Thiele, Judy Collins, Jill Godmilow, Arlo Guthrie, Lance Christensen, Moscow SCBWI critique group.

Dr. Miranda Wilson and the University of Idaho Preparatory Division faculty and families.

The Denver Philharmonic and the Washington-Idaho Symphony, for enthusiastically celebrating the release of this book.

Erin, Krista, Kayla, Isma, Patrick, Karen, Robert, Justin, Katie, Janet, John, Sammi, Brian, Brad, Angie, Sarah, Adam, Julia, Mom, Arbo, Tina, Jo.

Dad, you were a poet. I wish you could've seen the final book.

—Diane Worthey

SOURCE NOTES

Wilhelmina is amazed at what one little stick can do.
"The young girl was fascinated with the power wielded by the conductor of the band, later stating that she was 'amazed that a little stick could have such an influence on a group of people.'" Christensen, 1996.

The words go in one ear and out the other.
Nobody wants a woman conductor.
"The professor I loved the most in the whole world said to me, 'It won't work . . . it won't work . . . it won't work. Even if you get accepted into schools it won't work. Nobody wants a woman conductor.' How's that for your ego? Pretty bad, right? Well, it just went in one ear and out the other." Christensen, 1996.

Her friend tells her that if she takes the podium to conduct, the audience will throw rotten eggs at her.
"The audience is going to throw rotten tomatoes and rotten eggs at you." Antonia replied, "No, they won't." Collins and Godmilow, 1974.

He tells her that she will become a great conductor.
"Now you watch. No, Antonia, you are going to be a conductor. The renunciation is complete." Christensen, 1996.

"If nine, why not ninety?"
Collins and Godmilow, 1974.

But the symphony board says that no one will buy tickets.

"There are no more opportunities for you here," they say. "The board felt that the female aspect of the orchestra was its interesting feature." and "Since the orchestra had no capital that was that." Christensen, 1996.

BIBLIOGRAPHY

Ammer, Christine. *Unsung: A History of Women in American Music*. Portland: Amadeus Press, 2001.

"Antonia Brico's Triumph: First of Sex to Wield Baton Over NY. Philharmonic," *Newsweek*, August 1, 1938: vol. 12, no. 5, 21.

Bowers, Jane, and Judith Tick, eds. *Women Making Music: The Western Art Tradition, 1150–1950*. Chicago: University of Illinois Press, 1986: 355.

Brico, Antonia. "One Undeflected Step at a Time." Lecture, April 14, 1975. A Brico Collection, History Colorado (formerly Colorado Historical Society): box 1, folder 14, 4–5.

Christensen, Lance Eugene. *I Will Not Be Deflected from My Course: The Life of Dr. Antonia Brico*. MH Thesis, University of Colorado at Denver: Auraria Library Digital Collections, 2000.

Collins, Judy, and Jill Godmilow. *Judy Collins Presents: Antonia: Portrait of the Woman*. (film) 1974 by Rocky Mountain

Productions, 2015 Wildflower Records, LLC. Under exclusive license to Cleopatra Records, 11041 Santa Monica Blvd PMB 703, Los Angeles, CA 90025.

Collins, Judy. *Singing Lessons*. New York: Pocket Books, 1998.

Green, Lucy. *Music, Gender, Education*. Cambridge, UK: Cambridge University Press, 1997: 108-109.

Hardy, H.A. "Tin Mine Found," *Technical World Magazine*. September 1908: vol. 10–11, 663.

Jones, Isabel Morse. "Woman Scores as Conductor." *Los Angeles Times*, August 4, 1930. Accessed at http://latimes.newspapers.com.

Kendel, John C. "Antonia Brico Given Ovation at Denver Symphony's Concert." *Denver Post*, December 11, 1940.

Kozinn, Allan. "Antonia Brico, 87, A Conductor; Fought Barriers to Women in 30s." Obituary: *New York Times*, August 5, 1989.

"Miss Brico Triumphs as Berlin Conductor," *New York Times*, February 15, 1930, 14. Accessed at https://timesmachine.nytimes.com/timesmachine/1930/02/15/92076524.html?pageNumber=14

Sadie, Julie Anne and Samuel Rhian, eds. *The Norton/Grove Dictionary of Women Composers*. W.W. Norton & Company, 1995: 197, 439, 503–4.

University of California, "Certificate of Honorable Dismissal or Leave of Absence" issued to Wilhelmina Wolthuis. September 5, 1924. A Brico Collection, Historical Colorado (formerly Colorado Historical Society): box 7, folder 193.

Varnell, Jeanne. *Women of Consequence: The Colorado Women's Hall of Fame*. Boulder: Johnson Books, 1999: 145–146.

Wieland Howe, Sondra. *Women Music Educators in the United States: A History*. Lanham, Maryland: Scarecrow Press, Inc., 2014: vol. 8, 148.

Young, Allen. "Concert Gives Fine Bruckner." *Denver Post*, January 20, 1950: 22.

Websites

Marin Alsop's website: www.marinalsop.com/timeline/

Colorado Women's Hall of Fame: http://www.cogreatwomen. org/project/antonia-brico/

Encyclopaedia Brittanica: http://www.britannica.com/ biography/Antonia-Brico

International Musician: https://internationalmusician.org/ joann-falletta/

New York Philharmonic Digital Archives: https://archives.
nyphil.org/index.php/artifact/02b43575-8568-4445-
974b-e2a8bcb0ca65-0.1?search-type=singleFilter&search-
text=Antonia+Brico&search-dates-from=&search-dates-to=

Rhinegold Publishing: https://www.rhinegold.co.uk/
han-na-chang-meet-the-maestro/

Berlin Philharmonic: https://www.berliner-philharmoniker.de/
en/titelgeschichten/20172018/female-conductors/

Colorado Public Radio, CPR Classical blog: http://www.cpr.
org/classical/story/who-was-antonia-brico-and-why-did-the-
denver-philharmonic-name-its-stage-after-her

WXJR Public Radio: https://www.wqxr.org/story/133841-
american-woman-new-yorker-all-firsts-ulster-orchestras-
podium/

DIANE WORTHEY is a violinist in the Washington-Idaho Symphony and teaches violin and viola to all ages of students at the University of Idaho Preparatory Division. As a teenager growing up in Denver, Colorado, she performed in the Brico Symphony (now the Denver Philharmonic) under Maestra Brico. *In One Ear and Out the Other: Antonia Brico and Her Amazingly Musical Life* is Diane's first children's book.